I Believe
in the Resurrection
of the Body

I Believe
in the Resurrection
of the Body

Rubem Alves

Fortress Press   Philadelphia

Translated by L. M. McCoy

Translated from the Portuguese *Creio na ressurreição do corpo*, 2d edition copyright © 1984 by The Ecumenic Center of Documentation and Information, Rio de Janeiro, Brazil.

Scripture quotations are from the Revised Standard Version of the Bible, copyright 1946, 1952, © 1971, 1973 by the Division of Christian Education of the National Council of the Churches of Christ in the U.S.A. and are used by permission.

Excerpt from Friedrich Nietzsche, "Thus Spoke Zarathustra" in *The Portable Nietzsche*, ed. Walter Kaufmann (New York: The Viking Press, 1965) p. 204.

Excerpts from Walter Rauschenbusch, *Prayers of the Social Awakening* (Boston: The Pilgrim Press, 1910), pp. 47, 97, 107.

Illustrations by Guido Razzi are used by permission.

Library of Congress Cataloging-in-Publication Data

Alves, Rubem A., 1933–
  I believe in the resurrection of the body.

  Translation of: Creio na ressurreição do corpo.
  2nd ed.
  1. Meditations. 2. Prayers. I. Title.
BV4837.A4613 1986   242   85–16246
ISBN 0-8006-1885-8

1810G85   Printed in the United States of America   1–1885

CONTENTS

CELEBRATIONS OF THE RESURRECTION

The Christians included a strange declaration in their Creed. They said they believed in and wished for the resurrection of the body. As if the body were the only thing of any importance.

But could there be anything more important? Could there be anything more beautiful?

It is like a garden, where flowers and fruits grow.

The smile grows there,
generosity,
compassion,
the will to struggle,
hope;
the desire to plant gardens,
to bear children,
to hold hands and stroll,
to know . . .

And its ever-rising waters overflow, they run out of it, and the dry desert becomes a watered oasis. That's the way it is: in this body, so small, so ephemeral, a whole universe lives, and if it could, it would surely give its life for the life of the world. God's desire is revealed in our body. After all, what the doctrine of the incarnation whispers to us is that God, eternally, wants a body like ours. Have you ever thought about this? that at Christmas what is celebrated is our body, as something that God desires?

But the body is not only an overflowing spring: it is a welcoming lap.

The ear that hears the lament, in silence, without anything said.

The hand that grasps another.

The poem, which is the magic that transforms the world, putting in it invisible things, revealed only by the word.

The magical capacity to hear someone's tears, far away, never seen, and to weep also.

My body overflows and fertilizes the world.

The world overflows, and my body receives it.

So simple, so lovely.

But a strange thing happened. Something tempted us, and we began to look for God in perverse places.

We thought to find God where the body ends: and we made it suffer and transformed it into beast of burden, fulfiller of commands, machine for labor, enemy to be silenced, and we persecuted it in this way to the point of eulogizing death as the pathway to God, as if God preferred the smell of the tomb to the delights of Paradise.

And we became cruel, violent, we permitted exploitation and war. For if God is found beyond the body, anything can be done to the body.

I wrote these things as celebrations of the resurrection.

In the hope of the resurrection of the dead.

To exorcise death, which we ourselves feed with our flesh.

Invocations of joy and beauty.

Whoever is joyful and loves beauty fights better.

Resurrected bodies are more beautiful warriors because they bring in their hands the colors of the rainbow.

And so bodies are transformed into seed which impregnates the earth so the future can be born. . . .

Rubem Alves

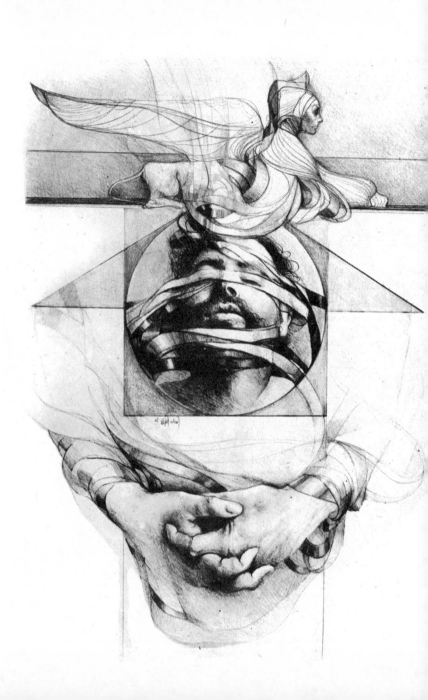

SACRAMENT

Now as they were eating, Jesus took bread, and blessed, and broke it, and gave it to the disciples and said, "Take, eat; this is my body." And he took a cup, and when he had given thanks he gave it to them, saying, "Drink of it, all of you; for this is my blood of the covenant, which is poured out for many for the forgiveness of sins. I tell you I shall not drink again of this fruit of the vine until that day when I drink it new with you in my Father's kingdom."

Matt. 26:26–29

And when the Lord smelled the pleasing odor, the Lord said in his heart, "I will never again curse the ground because of man, for the imagination of man's heart is evil from his youth; neither will I ever again destroy every living creature as I have done."

And God said, "This is the sign of the covenant which I make between me and you and every living creature that is with you, for all future generations: I set my bow in the cloud, and it shall be a sign of the covenant between me and the earth. When I bring clouds over the earth and the bow is seen in the clouds, I will remember my covenant which is between me and you and every living creature of all flesh; and the waters shall never again become a flood to destroy all flesh."

Gen. 8:21; 9:12–15

I have, in my yard, a lilac bush. It is in everything just like all
the other lilac bushes in the world. That delightful scent when
you crush its petals; white, with a drop of rose color, thou-
sands of little blossoms in season; and the countless bees that
gather and buzz around it. I like to stretch out in the hammock, near it, when the nights are cool and there is that
breeze. At times I find myself talking to the bush and I have
even thanked it for its leaves, as if it were aware. One never
knows for sure.

Just like all others except for one thing. It was my father who
gave me the little slip to plant, a cut branch, a long time ago.
My father is dead now. The lilac bush preserves his gesture.
As if, from the bush there come out strands of memory which
link me to someone who is no longer present. Threads, of
course, that no one sees. Only I see them. Or those to whom I
wish to reveal the secret. The space around that lilac bush is
magic—for me, who sees the threads. My friends, who don't
know the secret, smell the perfume, see the greenness. If I
should ask them about the bush they would tell me what they
see. They would go over that bit about the silent and faithful
presence: the lilac bush. But it wouldn't get beyond that. The
mouth is prisoner of the eyes. Tied down to the ground. Lacking the words that would let it soar. Only I, beginning with
the lilac bush, would be able to speak of an absence; someone
who is not there, who used to be. And from the plant I jump to
a face; and I remember smiles, joys, sorrows. That's why the

12

space around the lilac bush is magic. Memory makes imagination soar and fills the air with human things, which have to do with friendship and loyalty from many years of living together.

A lovely thing, this: that there should be things that are more than things, things that make us remember. The dried flower in a book. Sometimes a whiff of perfume you catch while walking in the street. And there, down deep, comes the strange sensation of being linked, by that perfume, to someone, some place far away, in the past. The ringing of a bell that carries me to worlds where I have never been. The crowing of a cock that comes to us from spaces that don't exist any more. Or a toy, an old doll, forgotten. A dish with the taste of longing remembrance. Things present which open to us the world of absences. Isn't that what longing remembrance is? To feel that something is lacking, someone, whom the heart desires, is far away. But absence alone is not enough. There are a lot of things which have been lost and left behind, of which we have no longing remembrance. It's because we didn't love them. Longing remembrance is born when there is *love* and *absence*.

When things awaken longing remembrance and cause the memory of love and the desire for return to grow in the heart, we say that they are *sacraments*. This is a sacrament: visible signs of an absence, symbols which make us think about return. Like what happened with Jesus who, just before his departure, carried out a memorial of longing remembrance and of awaiting. He gathered his friends, followers, broke the bread and gave it to them to eat, took the wine and drank it with them saying that after that would come separation and longing remembrance. They would be like a bride from whom the bridegroom is stolen. Time of tears, of waiting. And wherever they went they would find the signs of an immense

13

Absence. And the heart would become troubled, without rest. And each of their words would be transformed into a prayer, because prayer is the word stammering with desire.

The secret of the lilac bush is mine alone. The memories and the longing remembrance it awakens are mine alone. So that, near to it, there is always a sad sensation of loneliness.

Different with the bread and the wine. Nobody eats a meal alone. There is a breaking, a distributing, hands that touch, eyes that meet. And, in all this, a sensation as if it were a conspiracy. Conspiracy, lovely word of forgotten origins. Conspire, inspire-with, breathe with someone, together. Conspirators: they breathe the same air. Jesus and his disciples, eating the bread and drinking the wine, breathed the same air; bodies there, glued to one another; and also the desire and love—principally their desire and love. The meal is eaten, the magic appears, the invisible threads of longing remembrance and of hopeful waiting are cast forth, and, beginning from there, men and women who have in their eyes that sad-happy mark of longing remembrance and of hope clasp each others' hands. Just as it should be with anyone who loves and is far away and has nothing to hold except the dried flower, the poem, the memories, a word. That's how it is with the community of Christians, this thing that is called church: together, conspiring, hands joined, they eat the bread, drink the wine, and feel a longing remembrance/hope that has no end.

TO THINK ABOUT

Invent a symbol for whatever you love most. To whom would you choose to tell the secret of this symbol?

We live offering and exchanging symbols: clothing, the way we cut our hair, the way we speak, the pennant of a football team, a new refrigerator, as compared with the old one. They reveal who we are. Take your symbols. What do they say about you? How do others interpret your symbols? What symbols are shared in your house? Which ones are kept secret? Why?

Jesus began his ministry announcing a symbol. He proclaimed the Kingdom of God. And nobody asked him anything. It seems they all knew what he was talking about. What does the Old Testament say about the Kingdom of God? Isa. 2:4; 9:17; 10:33—11:10.

You and your friends. The church you attend. Other religious groups. What symbols characterize these groups of persons? Usually the most important symbols are those we are willing to spend the most money on. Look at your budget. And the budget of your church. "Where your treasure is, there will your heart be also."

What symbols bring you together with other persons, in a life decision? Are there symbols that make you happy? Symbols for which you would be willing to die?

To Pray

O, God: Just as the disciples heard Christ's words of promise and began to eat the bread and drink the wine in the suffering of a longing remembrance and in the joy of a hope, grant that we may hear your words, spoken in each thing of our everyday affairs. Coffee, on our table in the morning; the simple gesture of opening a door to go out, free; the shouts of children in the parks; a familiar song, sung by an unfamiliar face; a friendly tree that has not yet been cut down. May simple things speak to us of your mercy and tell us that life can be good. And may these sacramental gifts make us remember those who do not receive them, who have their lives cut, every day, in the bread absent from the table; in the door of the prison, the hospital, the welfare home that does not open; in the sad child, feet without shoes, eyes without hope; in the war hymns that glorify death; in the deserts where once there was life. Christ was also sacrificed. And may we learn that we participate in the saving sacrifice of Christ when we participate in the suffering of his little ones. Amen.

DESIRE

The wilderness and the dry land shall be glad,
  the desert shall rejoice and blossom;
like the crocus it shall blossom abundantly,
  and rejoice with joy and singing.
The glory of Lebanon shall be given to it,
  the majesty of Carmel and Sharon.
They shall see the glory of the Lord,
  the majesty of our God.

Strengthen the weak hands,
  and make firm the feeble knees.
Say to those who are of a fearful heart,
  "Be strong, fear not!
Behold, your God
  will come with vengeance,
with the recompense of God.
  He will come and save you."

Then the eyes of the blind shall be opened,
  and the ears of the deaf unstopped;
then shall the lame man leap like a hart,
  and the tongue of the dumb sing for joy.
For waters shall break forth in the wilderness,
  and streams in the desert;
the burning sand shall become a pool,

and the thirsty ground springs of water;
the haunt of jackals shall become a swamp,
the grass shall become reeds and rushes.

Isa. 35:1–7

He shall judge between the nations,
and shall decide for many peoples;
and they shall beat their swords into plowshares,
and their spears into pruning hooks;
nation shall not lift up sword against nation,
neither shall they learn war any more.

Isa. 2:4

For every boot of the tramping warrior in battle tumult
and every garment rolled in blood
will be burned as fuel for the fire.
For to us a child is born,
to us a son is given;
and the government will be upon his shoulder,
and his name will be called
"Wonderful Counselor, Mighty God,
Everlasting Father, Prince of Peace."

Isa. 9:5–6

Now after John was arrested, Jesus came into Galilee,
preaching the gospel of God, and saying, "The time is
fulfilled, and the kingdom of God is at hand; repent, and
believe in the gospel."

Mark 1:14–15

And if I should ask you to tell (to sing) your dreams of love?
What images would you offer to your traveling companions
as bread and wine? Those memories and hopes that call forth
a smile and that, if realized, would make the world a more

18

friendly place. If, as in children's stories, you were promised the fulfillment of one wish, just one, the most intense, most ardent, the one on which your life and death depended. Do you know what you would say? Or have you lost the memory of paradise, its desires forgotten, buried in the daily routine, mediocre and inexorable?

We are that which we love.

Neither larger nor smaller than the size of the objects of our desire. And that is why Christians become known by revealing to each other their dreams. To dream is to see love and desires transformed into symbols, words. It should not be frightening, then, that God, who is love, speaks to us through our *dreams*. And may we, from our part, speak to God through *prayer*, which is nothing more than the confession of our dream of love before the altar.

To take the bread and wine of the eucharist is to speak of a great promise of love, which was among us, which went away, and whose return we await. "Come, Lord Jesus": prayer of the primitive Christians, confession of longing remembrance, sigh of waiting/hope. That's why it is good to talk about him; on him depend our deepest desires.

Have you ever seen those screens on which carpets are woven? In the end, the work done, the screens are not even seen. That's because in the end they were metamorphosed in the place where beauty took form. Without the screen, there would be no beauty; the lines would go every which way, in the air. But to the degree that the lines construct the designs, the screen progressively disappears. Beauty, gracious gift of something, must become invisible to be given.

Christ, the place of our desire. Like the screen, invisible. John the Baptist, intense passion, eyes on the future, which is the place of hope, of the advent of love. In prison. Powerless. His days numbered. And the question arises as to whether the whole thing might not have been a big mistake. Possible that he had been deceived. He sends some of his friends to put the question to Jesus. And he gave no answer, went around passing his hands, his eyes, his words, desire, over poor and suffering persons, and the magic began to happen, tears became smiles, suddenly. And he sent the emissaries back to say that in some way no one could explain, in that man, Jesus of Nazareth, the things for which people's hearts longed, the absences for which they felt longing remembrance, the desires of their nostalgia were becoming reality. The Kingdom of God is arrived, and its face is the happiness of humankind. Like the carpet. God, invisible as God, becomes visible as desire, and becomes thing, person, gesture: joined hands; a child playing in a water fountain; the poor who eat bread; the lonely one with someone to talk to; the weak one who no longer needs to shrink, crouching; plants that are born; fences that are torn down; prisons are opened; the lame leap; deserts are transformed into gardens; the aged, without fear of old age. And the instruments of suffering and death, evil inventions, become a bonfire—and there are the boots and the uniforms stained with blood, it's of little importance that their manufacture and sale make us richer and are good for the economy—the resurrection of the body, the smiles of pleasure, liberty, fields covered with wheat and beans, swaying in the breeze, and vines loaded with grapes, the final expulsion of fear, eternal life.

Something unprecedented, this thing that Christians are beginning to say, that to talk about God is to talk about human beings, that the glory of God is found in happy people, salvation. God naked, revealed, the veil removed. And then the fright comes, because what appears is the body of a man, which is the body of all, in which our longing remembrances and nostalgia are interlaced in a tapestry of desire and of love.

World, body of Christ,
Body of Christ, love made real;
Jesus, joy of humankind

And it is about this tapestry of desires, woven on the body of Christ, that Christians talk.

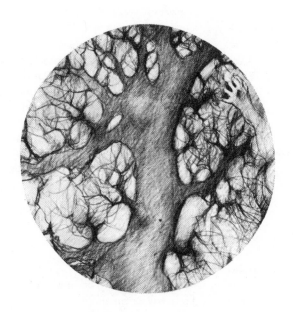

TO THINK ABOUT

What are your desires? And if you had to choose just one of them? "Purity of heart is to desire one thing only" (Søren Kierkegaard). "You shall die because of your small virtues" (Friedrich Nietzsche).

Among your desires, have you not forgotten to list those that are considered "unworthy" or "impure"? It is important to face up to them. We are in front of a mirror.

When you pray, what do you offer to God as your most intense desire?

The Kingdom of God: what desires are contained in this symbol? Try to talk about the desires contained in the symbol of the Kingdom, what they contain of joy, of life, of laughter. And say this to a child, a slum dweller, a migrant worker, an unemployed person.

Talk about the desires that the people in your church exchange with each other. Do people confess their desires to each other in churches?

To Pray

O Lord, our God,
give us the grace to desire you with all our heart; and may
  our desire lead us to seek you and to find you;
and, having found you, may we be able to love you.
And, loving you, may we hate those sins from which you
  have redeemed us.

Saint Anselm, *Proslogion*

LONGING REMEMBRANCE

Blessed are the poor in spirit, for theirs is the kingdom of heaven.
Blessed are those who mourn, for they shall be comforted.
Blessed are the meek, for they shall inherit the earth.
Blessed are those who hunger and thirst for righteousness, for they shall be satisfied.
Blessed are the merciful, for they shall obtain mercy.
Blessed are the pure in heart, for they shall see God.
Blessed are the peacemakers, for they shall be called sons of God.
Blessed are those who are persecuted for righteousness' sake, for theirs is the kingdom of heaven.

Matt. 5:3–10

The difference is the same as with my lilac bush. When I look at it I see things no one else sees. And it is this, these different things, invisible, that dwell in the world of memory and of hopes, that make the world magic/secret, that throb around the little tree without anyone suspecting. So much so that they think it is just one among many, and that it can be given, with a little cut slip to plant.

And we talk about this mysterious name, planted, two thousand years ago, that for some means nothing, a name among others, evoking nothing at all from the void. Sounding brass, tinkling cymbal. But we discover that something different happens when we pronounce it with longing remembrance that comes from the depths.

We must not forget longing remembrance.

It makes all the difference.

God dwells in longing remembrance, there where love and absence are found together.

Which reminds me of a brother, with a strange name, Kierkegaard, who invented a parable to talk about magic, about the nostalgia that he, like us, was feeling.

Two men went to pray. One of them, a baptized Christian, Christian also in speech and habits, went to the sanctuary of the true God, place of right names and orthodox ideas, where he knelt down and prayed.

Far away from there, a pagan who had never heard the names that are sacred to us and knew nothing of the God of Abraham, Isaac, and Jacob, Jesus Christ, went also to the sanctuary. Except that there in that place there were no symbols of the true God. They were idols. But the Christian, kneeling before the correct symbols, repeated those things that are repeated, without the heart trembling, without our son, only and loved son, being placed on the altar of sacrifice. He spoke without longing remembrance, without pain. The poor pagan, without the help of the true symbols, knelt before the false gods. But without consequence, because there remained in the depths of his soul an endless nostalgia, witness that no idol could satisfy, witness of a prayer that was not spoken: "Thy kingdom come . . ." And the parable ends by

24

saying that the Christian, kneeling before God, worshipped an idol; and the pagan, kneeling before an idol, worshipped the true God. Longing remembrance made all the difference.

Strange thing. Longing remembrance, we cannot create it by an act of will. It is born, without our willing it, when the mysterious wind of the Spirit blows. And we know that the thing is of the Spirit by the new things that begin to become visible. The eyes are changed. The heart, too. And it is because the heart becomes different that the eyes begin to see things that no one else sees. They are invisible. And because we see invisible things, others think we are mad. It is not a question of just looking at Jesus all the time. The ones who killed him saw him better than we do. He is not flesh, and he is not blood. He is mystery. As if he became transparent and we began to see the whole world through him. "Behold all things are remade. They become new." I have a painting by Salvador Dali, The Last Supper. The upper room, Jesus and the disciples, the broken bread, the translucent red wine. It happens that the painter perceived that without transparency there is no eucharist. And he made the walls of the upper room enormous, of glass, as they never really were, but as they are in the magic of longing remembrance. And, from the simplicity of the eucharist, the eye plunges outward, seeing the sea, the beaches, the mountains, the world, the universe, all of this transfigured by the embrace of an enormous human/divine body, arms open, welcoming all to the table. This is the question: the other things, desired, which our longing remembrance of Christ makes us see.

"The essential is invisible to the eye," said the fox to the little prince. The shy rose that I watered is different from all the proud roses grown in chemical fertilizer that no one loved. And it is words that make the difference. That's why Jesus did not give just bread and wine. To eat was not enough. It is

25

necessary to see with new eyes. To eat to see better. It was for this that he performed the magic, mixing into the food the words of love and of promise, to cure our blindness. And then he said that the food was something other than what it appeared to be. Bread and wine, body and blood, aperitif of a return. Without the magic of words we would be like animals, no better than pigs. We would live immersed in an opaque world of things, destitute of transparency, without seeing the invisible, without memory of a loss, and without longing remembrance; and without the hope that is born of longing remembrance.

A common longing remembrance,
This is our sacrament: bread and wine.
We feel longing remembrance together.
This makes us brothers and sisters.

With our hands joined we pray out of nostalgia for the Kingdom of God, the realization of the body of Christ. And we repeat the words that each Christian, in birth pangs, repeats as an invocation: "Blessed are the . . ."

TO THINK ABOUT

Longing remembrance of Christ: what is it? Longing for God? Have you ever felt it? How? When? For what things do you have longing remembrance? Think about them. See them. Sense the smells, the forms, the colors. How do you link your longing remembrances to your faith in Christ?

Is the church a community of longing remembrance? When people pray, "Thy Kingdom come," can it be that they feel that nostalgia of someone who has lost a loved one? What evidence is there that the church is the community that lives from longing remembrances of Christ?

Meditate on your experience of prayer, in the light of Soren Kierkegaard's parable. One of the indications that we love someone is our capacity to remain silent, saying nothing, with that person. Our experience of prayer: silence, speech? Speech that comes from the depths?

To Pray

O thou, omnipotent good,
that carest for each of us as if only for him,
and carest for all, as if there were only one!
Blessed is the man that loves thee . . .
I see that things pass,
that others take their place,
but thou dost never pass.
O God, my Father, supreme good,
beauty of all beautiful things,
in thy hands I place all that I received from thee,
that I may lose nothing.

Thou hast made me for thyself,
and my heart is restless,
until it finds its rest in thee.

Saint Augustine, *Confessions*

GOD'S SMILING FACE

Therefore I tell you, do not be anxious about your life, what you shall eat or what you shall drink, nor about your body, what you shall put on. Is not life more than food, and the body more than clothing? Look at the birds of the air: they neither sow nor reap nor gather into barns, and yet your heavenly Father feeds them. Are you not of more value than they? And which of you by being anxious can add one cubit to his span of life? And why are you anxious about clothing? Consider the lilies of the field, how they grow; they neither toil nor spin; yet I tell you, even Solomon in all his glory was not arrayed like one of these. But if God so clothes the grass of the field, which today is alive and tomorrow is thrown into the oven, will he not much more clothe you, O men of little faith? Therefore do not be anxious, saying, "What shall we eat?" or "What shall we drink?" or "What shall we wear?" For the Gentiles seek all these things; and your heavenly Father knows that you need them all. But seek first his kingdom and his righteousness, and all these things shall be yours as well.

Therefore do not be anxious about tomorrow, for tomorrow will be anxious for itself. Let the day's own trouble be sufficient for the day.

Matt. 6:25–34

God dwells in longing remembrance, there where love and absence are found together. To sense God? To have communion with him? It is to feel nostalgia for the Kingdom, to groan with the whole creation, feeling within ourselves the future which is growing, growing, like pregnancy.

There, in the land of longing remembrance, we make our habitation.

We are immigrants, without rest, without a stopping place, always on the road. There is no place to rest our head. Like plants torn up, roots visible, out of dry ground. Exiles, we build our nests in trees of the future. It is thus that, on the trail, we build our rude altars and burn our sacrifices (Romans 12), chanting as a hymn the name of this endless longing, Jesus Christ. We beg him to give bread and wine to our nostalgia, telling us about his hopes, the free, joyful, fraternal, playful bodies in the Kingdom of God, the beatitudes made real.

And he begins.

But then come astonishment and alarm. We expected that he would talk about divine things. But he talks only about human things. Little ones. About the delights of heaven and the terrors of hell only a discreet murmur, if not silence. But he speaks of the tranquility of the birds, the beauty of the wild flowers, the sun that rises on the good and the evil, the rain, as well. And he tells us about children whose games are dancing and playing flutes; he goes to parties, introduces in the midst of the celebration his own wine; he speaks of purity of heart; points out that life is more important than laws; is saddened with our anguish, fear of the future, desire to run things and be seen, wish to be more important; he prefers the company of the marginal and the despised to the bowing and scraping of those who use sacred deodorants; he laughs at the powerful

(even knowing its risks); rather the adulterer who sinned for love than those who, virtuous from age and from fear, stand with rocks in their hands; he eats and drinks with ordinary people, speaks in an enigmatic manner, knowing that pearls should not be cast before swine (to the pigs, slop); he tells frightful stories in which the villains of real life always appear as heroes and the heroes of real life always appear as villains. But these are things of this world, about men and women, children and old people, animals and trees. Right. He talks about our world. About life. About our bodies. He talks about smiles and tears.

And we shake with fear.

Why? Because we want to be even more spiritual than God. Where Jesus Christ speaks to us of life, of the body, of the world, we would have preferred that he talked to us of the secrets that lie beyond the tomb.

The humanity of God bugs us.
That's right: the humanity of God. Something the first Christians discovered with great apprehension. I'd better correct myself. It's not that the Christians, after becoming solidly Christian, discovered the humanity of God as *something else* to talk about, something that could be added to their theological ideas. The truth is the opposite. It was when they discovered that to talk about God it is necessary to quit talking about God and to talk about a person, a face, a life. That's when they became Christians.

God, to talk about himself, became man. To talk about God is to talk about a man. The word was made flesh. Our brother. One of us. He was born, lived, died.

If someone should ask me, "Who are you?" do you know

what I would say? First, I'll tell you what I would not say. I would not talk about my intestines, or my teeth, or my blood pressure. Do you know why? These things don't help us to smile at each other. But it would be completely different if I talked about my dreams, the things I like, longings and hopes. In talking about desires, we might discover that we can become friends, walk along together. Or maybe discover that we have nothing in common, that our commitments are different. That's the way it always is. "How shall two walk together if they are not in agreement?" And the strong and the weak take different roads, those who want to hold on to the present, and those who want a new world to arise out of this present.

We are not the *substance* of what we are made of: flesh, bones, blood. We are our desires, nostalgia, the love that is born of this flesh by the miraculous blowing of a vagrant wind. As if the Spirit of God had made us pregnant. "Whoever is born of the flesh is flesh. You must be born again."

Sometimes we would like to know what God is made of. To know his sacred substance. And many pages of theological books and catechisms have been written to describe the marvelous properties of God's flesh: spirit, invisible, omnipotent, omniscient, omnipresent. And with words like these we write essays on sacred anatomy and physiology.

Waste of time. The Christians discovered that this man, Jesus of Nazareth, is God's answer to the question "Who are you?" And he answers us, not with a treatise on anatomy/physiology, but by telling us about his desires. God is love. And he tells us about his dream of love. He places it alive, among us. Jesus of Nazareth is God's desire. He is his choice. A lovelier, more beautiful, more delightful thing there can not be.

33

"What do you want to be when you grow up?"—that's what we say to children. If, without irreverence, we could ask God the same thing, he would say, "But you still don't know? Haven't I told you? I told you and you didn't listen. You thought I was joking. Yes, I want to be Jesus of Nazareth. I am Jesus of Nazareth. I am an ordinary man. I am all ordinary people. Especially the suffering, the weak, the abandoned. 'Whenever you did it to one of these my little ones, you did it to me.' There is nothing better than to be a man, a woman, a child. No, I don't want fleshless human beings. Let the bodies be resurrected. No, I don't want the end of the world, of the animals, trees, oceans, breeze. All of this is very good. Let everything be redeemed. The earth will yet be a place of laughter and play. That's what I want, this is my desire. And that's why my Spirit continues to be a praying Spirit. To pray is to speak with desire, with love. And I myself intercede, with my desire and my body, body of Jesus and body of all who suffer, the whole creation, groaning, in birth pangs, waiting, hopeful."

TO THINK ABOUT

Do a little exercise, one which demands great honesty. Say the word "God" and look at the images it brings to your mind.

Now turn the exercise around. Think about things you really like. And try to put them together with God, with religion. What result did you get? Does your God make you smile?

Christians "have called 'God' what was contrary to them and gave them pain." Friedrich Nietzsche said this, impressed with the lack of happiness, the seriousness, the lack of joy of living that could be seen in church people. What do you think about this?

God's desire is salvation; salvation is deep joy for life, for body, for nature. All of this related to the promise of the Kingdom of God, whose announcement is the good news, the gospel. What does it mean, then, to evangelize?

Happiness has to do with the body and with the spirit. Redeemed body implies health, liberty, justice. These are things within our reach, part of our task as gardeners. The spirit, on the other hand, is fed by the symbols we share. Among them are memories and hopes. Think about the task of the church as minister or shepherdess of gladness.

To Pray

O God, I remember those who can have no joy today!
parents whose children died;
unemployed;
those in prisons, being tortured;
the ill, in pain;
old people, lonely;
peasants, landless;
Indians, living the last days of their people;
those who have nothing to eat.
In some way, may the gentle breath of the Spirit cause hope
   to shine in their hearts, and may they have the courage to
   struggle for a better world,
sacrament of the Kingdom of God.
I remember, also, those who can have no joy because they
   are under the domination of idols,
possessed by evil spirits,
those who think only about their profit, and so exploit the
   poor;
those who can with impunity use arms and violence, and so
   perfume their bodies and mock rights;
those who because they think only about themselves, are
   unable to feel the sweet tenderness of solidarity with those
   who suffer.
Help me to rejoice in that sadness from which there springs
   forth nostalgia for the Kingdom of God and to hate the
   sadness of those who have eyes only for themselves.
And may the sad ones of your Kingdom never lack the sweet
   sacrament of the smile of God. Amen.

THE THINGS THAT GOD LOVES

Beloved, let us love one another; for love is of God, and he who loves is born of God and knows God. He who does not love does not know God; for God is love. No man has ever seen God; if we love one another, God abides in us and his love is perfected in us.

1 John 4:7–8, 12

There is no fear in love, but perfect love casts out fear. For fear has to do with punishment, and he who fears is not perfected in love. We love, because he first loved us. If any one says, "I love God," and hates his brother, he is a liar; for he who does not love his brother whom he has seen, cannot love God whom he has not seen.

1 John 4:18–20

Jesus of Nazareth is God's desire,
her greatest dream transformed into body,
her confession of love among us.

"Who sees me sees the Father."

It so happens that we only feel longing remembrance of one who is absent.
Every desire is witness that something is lacking.

That's why to speak of longing remembrance and of desire is prayer: to invoke, to call, so that the distant comes near; the absent, present; the invisible, visible; hope, reality; pregnancy, child in arms; seed, flower; hate, love; death, life.

Jesus is God's prayer petition. . . .
God also hopes, God also desires.
This is what is frightening and scary in this God who is seen deep in the eyes of Jesus of Nazareth: God crucified, sacrificed, God pregnant-woman, in the gestation of a new world, redemption, tears, God who weeps. And it is about this that the body of a crucified one speaks to us: the pain of waiting. God is the victim: it is necessary to wait. Beatitudes: song of the *not yet*. "In hope we are saved. But who hopes still has not seen."

Jesus is speech about the things that God loves, things for which Jesus became victim and wants to cause to be born. To speak about herself God does not speak about herself: she speaks of the objects of her desire.

This is a lovely thing, that the heart of God should be a human person. That God's substance should be a people body. That the body of God should be the entire universe, creation, child which God's desire begot.

God, in herself, behind her human face? Nobody knows what she is. "No one has seen God. It is his Son, from next to his heart, who has revealed him."

Reveal, remove the veil.
And when the veil goes, what is seen?

The mysteries of divinity that make us tremble? The fire that consumes? Secrets from beyond the tomb? The billows of the storm, from before creation itself? The mighty wind that blew? The shadows?

Perhaps, for some, disappointment.

They wanted to see the "mysterium tremendum," wanted to tremble, before the mystery.

But God prefers smiles. And she prohibits talking about her. The name of God cannot be pronounced. Reduced to silence. Expelled from speech.

"You shall not make for yourselves images. . . ."
Names are images, too.

Worse than the clay idols. Clay idols we leave in the sanctuaries. But names, we carry them everywhere, in the words of our mouth or in the silent words of our nocturnal machinations.

The veil is removed. And there is the heart of God.

Heart: mirror in which mankind and the universe appear transfigured by the magic of love, like the utopia of a new world, to come. Not another world. Not another creation. In God's universe, nothing is lost. God does not abandon the work of her hands; does not change her mind. Everything continues to be very good. It must remain, forever. And she, potter, takes the clay in her hands, and starts over.

To speak about God's desires, this we can do. Speak about Jesus of Nazareth. We talk about God being silent about God, the prohibited name. We talk about God by talking about the future which dwells, silent, within our own sighs and the groans of all those who suffer: the end of fear, of pain, of

39

tears, of deserts, of armaments, of prisons. Kingdom of God, *for us*, for God herself who chose to be us.
Mystery of the Trinity, supreme symbol:
God, forbidden name,
is, eternally, Son, Jesus of Nazareth, who breathes invisible and through all spaces and for all time, the breath of life and of hope: the Spirit.

So, to speak of God is not to speak of God. It is to speak of her desire for us. That is all we know: God for us, "pro nobis," human face.

How to talk about God, without pronouncing her name? The eye, to see the world, can not see itself. The eye has to be transparent. And it is when we forget her that we are most under the grace of God's miracle: to see through the eye, without seeing the eye; see the clouds and fields, the persons and the gardens. But, what about the eye? There is no need to talk about it. Above all, it is necessary that we not see it.

No one has ever seen God.
So that we may see through her.
And speaking, not about God in her mysteries, but in the revelation of her desire; paradise, holy city, promise, redemption, pure joy, resurrection, creation distributed as a sacrament, fraternization with all people.

TO THINK ABOUT

Think about the things that God loves. Read the story of creation in Genesis: "And God saw that everything was very good. . . ." What was very good? God rested from her labors. A great thing! She rested, "seeing." Do you know how to see? Most people don't know how to see, or hear, or feel. Routines blind us. Today, before going to sleep, set aside a little time for this exercise. It is simple. Develop phrases which begin with the affirmation: "Here and now . . . "

"Here and now I am hearing the crickets,

I am hearing the breeze,

I am seeing a violet, which was there,

but which I did not see,

I am sensing my body."

What good is this exercise? To call us back from our routines to things which, right in front of us, we lose. Learn to cultivate silence in order to hear better.

To talk about God is to speak of *God's promises* of joy to humankind. Do you agree with this statement? Give your reasons.

Saint Augustine said that what makes us members of the same community is the fact of loving the same things. What is the greatest love of your ecclesial community? What is your greatest love? Are there other communities that love the same things that you do? Other communities participating in the same Kingdom banquet? Isn't it strange that, most of the time, we consider what people think, and not what they love, to be most important?

To Pray

O Christ, you bade us pray for the coming of your Father's
Kingdom, when his righteous will would be done on earth.
We keep your words, but we forget their meaning, so that
your great hope has been weakened, almost come to an end,
in your Church. We praise you for those souls on whom
your Spirit breathed, in all ages, so that they might see, far
off, the shining city of God, and by faith left the advantages
of the present to follow that vision. There is joy in knowing
that the hope of these solitary hearts is becoming, today, the
transparent faith of millions. Help me, O God, in the
courage of faith, that we may seize that which has now come
so near, that God's joyful day may finally be born. As we
were capable of dominating Nature, for love of riches, help
us to transfigure the relationships between persons, so that
we may establish justice and build a world of brothers. For
what does it profit a nation to become great and rich, if it
loses the sense of the living God and the joy of human
brotherhood? Help us to live by truths and not by lies, to
build our common life on the eternal foundations of justice
and of love, to quit propping up the cracked walls of the
house of injustice by the use of legalized force and cruelty.
Help us to make the welfare of all the supreme law of this
land so that our family may grow, strong and secure, in the
love of all citizens. Bring down from his throne the god
Profit, who endlessly chews up the body of men, and put in
its place your throne, O Christ, for you died that men may
live. Show your wandering children the way which leads
from the City of Destruction to the City of Love, and bring
to reality the aspirations of the prophets of humanity. Our
Master, once more your faith is our prayer: "Thy Kingdom
come! Thy will be done on earth!"

Walter Rauschenbusch, *Prayers of the Social Awakening*

THE GARDEN

*In the day that the Lord God made the earth and the
heavens, when no plant of the field was yet in the earth and
no herb of the field had yet sprung up—for the Lord God
had not caused it to rain upon the earth, and there was no
man to till the ground; but a mist went up from the earth and
watered the whole face of the ground—then the Lord God
formed man of dust from the ground, and breathed into his
nostrils the breath of life; and man became a living being.
And the Lord God planted a garden in Eden, in the east; and
there he put the man whom he had formed. And out of the
ground the Lord God made to grow every tree that is
pleasant to the sight and good for food, the tree of life also in
the midst of the garden, and the tree of the knowledge of
good and evil.*

Gen. 2:4b–9

*So the Lord God caused a deep sleep to fall upon the man,
and while he slept took one of his ribs and closed up its place
with flesh; and the rib which the Lord God had taken from
the man he made into a woman and brought her to the man.
And the man and his wife were both naked, and were not
ashamed.*

Gen. 2:21–22, 25

For lo, the winter is past,
the rain is over and gone.
The flowers appear on the earth,
the time of singing has come,
and the voice of the turtledove
is heard in our land.
The fig tree puts forth its figs,
and the vines are in blossom;
they give forth fragrance.
Arise, my love, my fair one,
and come away.

Song of Sol. 2:11–13

Just as the eye is the eye only if it is transparent, God gives herself, transparent and invisible, so that through her we may see life with new eyes.

The same thing happens with the light of the sun. Straight in the eyes, it dazzles and blinds, but on our backs it is gracious and smiling, and from it there spills out the rainbow. And visible beauty is born, gift of invisible light.

It's that way with God, too, invisible, at our backs, hidden, absconditus as the theologians said in the old days, going along giving herself to us through the things she makes us see.

It is not a question of seeing God.
It is a question of seeing with God.
"And God saw that everything was very good."
Everything?
That's right.
Universe, around a garden.

The astronomers of the past used to say, "Everything revolves about the earth." Other more modern ones said, "Everything revolves about the sun." In either case, everything revolves

44

about something, little or big, cold or hot, and we have no importance. But God said, with a smile and playfully, "Everything revolves about a garden. Universe-garden."

Garden: gracious friendly nature.

Friendship between humans and things, humans and animals, humans and plants. And shapes, colors, bird sounds, sounds of insects and of the wind come together to make everything beautiful and the soul happy.

How does a garden appear?

First of all, there must be a gardener. There must be a desire. The imagination must soar.

There is the hard, dry land, thorns, the sun that punishes the cracked soil, the springs that don't exist. Brute nature, improper for life, enemy, hostile, sinister. People come, look, their eyes suffer. Because they do not see just with their eyes. They see with the soul, desire. Everything could be different. And they dream. Imagination soars. The garden, fountains, shade, flowers, breeze, the locust chattering in the afternoons and the birds in the mornings; nights are friendly because the fences keep the wild animals away; feet can run unshod because there are no thorns; and bodies are uncovered to the caress of the breeze and the play of the fountains. Imagination calls to the body, mobilizes the hands, and work comes, which transforms suffering into smiles, deserts into gardens, deserted places into pleasant living spaces. Home, friendly city. City, nothing more than a garden for a lot of people. That's why God's desire jumps from Paradise to the Holy City. There's not a lot of difference. Garden, human space, where life can reign. City, *polis*—and the forgotten meaning of political: people, imagination in flight, hands joined, building friendly places, habitations, paradises, where there should be no unnecessary meaning nor provoked tears, because the compatibility of human beings with nature accompanies the compatibility between human beings. God, builder of gardens. And she saw that everything was very good. To make gardens is to play. Joy. Sweat that satisfies the soul's thirst. And when the hand removes the stones and rips up the thorn bushes, songs are heard and clouds dance and everything proclaims that the glory of God is the happiness of humankind. God shines when people laugh.

"Sursum corda! All matter is Spirit" (Fernando Pessoa).
How strange what orientals, our ancestors, dared to think.
And Spirit *desires* to become thing, matter.

"And God said: Let there be . . ." And she created
fountains,
fruits, streams,
clouds, mountains, stars,
beetles, shamrocks, orchids, fish,
algae, shellfish, daisies, rabbits, words,
gestures, altars, seeds of plants and animals and people, the women became pregnant, children were born, cried, played, and a butterfly rose in flight. . . .

The voice of God echoed, omnipotent desire, through the shadows of the abyss, and from nothing the world was made.

Matter, things, the Spirit offering itself to the hands, the mouth, the eyes, the skin. God gives herself. God gives herself *this way*.

Creation. The Spirit gives us the creation, sacrament, garden. She gives humans as body, naked body, male body, female body, bodies that need hide nothing, everything was good, the eyes were good, image of God. Body, gift of God, destined for eternity. A pain that touches the body touches also the apple of God's eye. God senses through human bodies. She needs us. And God walks through the garden, in the evening breeze, appearing in the colorful, friendly spaces of the sacrament world. And she assumes body, is born of woman, hungers, thirsts, weeps, walks, sleeps, dies.

"And God saw that everything was very good."

And what God wishes should be destined forever.

TO THINK ABOUT

To be God's companion, co-creator. In the creation, God made a garden, pleasant place so that men, women, children (and, who knows, plants and animals) could feel happy. Think about your work: in what way is it an extension of God's gardening?

In thinking about work, those who can *choose* a profession usually think about what they can earn. How are orientation toward profit, toward earning, and toward garden building related?

Is profit good for garden making? Profit: destruction of the forest, pollution; the city transformed into a mass of crowded apartments, traffic; workers transformed into merchandise (each strike is a discussion about the price of a commodity, the rent of the worker's body!).

Garden: so that humans might be happy.

Rich country, great power: happier people?

Do you know of other cultures, older, poorer, that built more friendly and tranquil gardens than our cement jungles and our deserts?

Where are the churches to be found in this project of transforming the world into a garden? Note that paradise is not just the story of something that happened and was lost forever. Paradise lost should be regained. Memory is also a hope.

What wild animals invade our paradise turning it into a nest of snakes and of birds of prey?

To Pray

O God, we thank you for this universe, our home; and for its vastness and richness, the exuberance of life which fills it and of which we are part. We praise you for the vault of heaven and for the winds, pregnant with blessings, for the clouds which navigate and for the constellations, there so high. We praise you for the oceans and for the fresh streams, for the endless mountains, the trees, the grass under our feet. We praise you for our senses, to be able to see the morning splendor, to hear the songs of lovers, to smell the beautiful fragrance of the spring flowers. Give us, we pray you, a heart that is open to all this joy and all this beauty, and free our souls of the blindness that comes from preoccupation with the things of life, and of the shadows of passions, to the point that we no longer see nor hear, not even when the bush at the roadside is afire with the glory of God. Give us a broader sense of communion with all living things, our sisters, to whom you gave this world as a home along with us. We remember with shame that in the past we took advantage of our greater power and used it with unlimited cruelty, so much so that the voice of the Earth, which should have arisen to you as a song was turned into a moan of suffering. May we learn that living things do not live just for us, that they live for themselves and for you, and that they love the sweetness of life as much as we do, and serve you, in their place, better than we do in ours. When our end arrives and we can no longer make use of this world, and when we have to give way to others, may we leave nothing destroyed by our ambition or deformed by our ignorance, but may we pass along our common heritage more beautiful and more sweet, without having removed from it any of its fertility and joy, and so may our bodies return in peace to the womb of the great mother who nourished us and our spirits enjoy perfect life in you.

Walter Rauschenbusch, *Prayers of the Social Awakening*

THE BODY

Then God said, "Let us make man in our image, after our likeness; and let them have dominion over the fish of the sea, and over the birds of the air, and over the cattle, and over all the earth, and over every creeping thing that creeps upon the earth." So God created man in his own image, in the image of God he created him; male and female he created them.

Gen. 1:26–27

And the Word became flesh and dwelt among us, full of grace and truth; we have beheld his glory, glory as of the only Son from the Father.

John 1:14

"I believe in the resurrection of the body."

From the Apostles' Creed

God made us bodies.
God made himself body. Took on flesh,
Body: image of God.
Body: our destiny, God's destiny.
That's good.
Eternal divine solidarity with human flesh.
Nothing more worthy.
The body is not destined to be elevated to spirit.

It is the Spirit which chooses to make itself visible, in the body.

Body: realization of the Spirit: its hands, eyes, words, gestures of love.

Body: womb where God is formed. Mary, pregnant, Jesus, silent fetus, waiting protected, in the warmth of a woman's belly.

Jesus: God's body among us.
Body given to human beings.
Body for bodies, as flesh and blood, bread and wine.

And the body of God, Jesus Christ, expands, fills out, occupies the entire universe: "present in all places, even in the very smallest leaf, in each created thing, within and without, around it and within its sinews, beneath and above, before and behind . . ." (Martin Luther)

The body is the gracious Spirit, capable of smiling, capable of becoming pregnant, procreating, dying of love.

It is right there, in the body, that God and humankind meet.

Because Jesus of Nazareth, God for us, God with us, is supportive God, in our garden, as body, forever.

Strange that we should close our eyes to pray.
Fear of the body? Fleeing the body, the garden, to a spirit, hidden from the body, hidden in the garden?
Think: what would be your reaction if, after you had chosen the most delicate flower or most precious gift for someone you love, yes, what would your reaction be if that someone received the gift with eyes closed? Should refuse to see, smell,

taste, touch? There are moments in which we do not want the loved one to look at us. They should look at the gift. That's where our love is. To close the eyes to the gift is the same as not wanting the gift to be a gift, sacrament, symbol of love.

But we close our eyes to pray.

Doesn't the garden please us?

Are we looking for God outside the garden?

Can we not see the signs of goodness and of beauty that are still there?

We close our eyes and look within, in search of a spirit. But God's Spirit is in the things, the bodies, the creation, and principally in the laughter and the moans that come out of the children and those who suffer. A cup of water, a toy, a lily, a bird, a germinating seed, the bread and wine, eyes that weep, hand that rejects violence, body that places itself in between in the defense of the innocent, deep faces of gentleness, the sun that shines, the heavens full of stars, the silence on the face of the oppressed, inheritors of the earth.

"I believe in the resurrection of the body. . . ."

Body forever; face of the Spirit.

Thirsting body,

sick body,

migrant body,

hungry body,

body in prison.

"When you did it to one of these my little ones, you did it to me. . . ."

Body: sanctuary, altar, host.

Holy of holies.

The Spirit loves,

the love becomes garden,

bodies,

which love each other in the garden;

54

garden of the Spirit,
Jesus of Nazareth,
who became bread and wine,
body distributed
for more love:
seed of the Universe-garden,
body of God,
Christ.
Us.
I.

TO THINK ABOUT

In the text of the meditation there is a short quotation from Martin Luther in which he speaks of the universal presence of Christ in all *things*. Have you ever thought about this? Persons: presences of Christ. Things: presences of Christ.

Luther refers also to the creation (nature, persons) as masks of Christ: Christ hidden, anonymous, there inside. What are the practical consequences of this for our life? Our relationship with nature, with children, old people, parents, one's own offspring, children, subordinates?

Beginning with the thought that the body is sacred and that whatever is done to anyone's body is done directly to God, draw out the consequences for:

a. Our use/irresponsible abuse of nature;

b. Agriculture that enriches the nation and does not feed the hungry;

c. Cruel treatment of prisoners, of foreigners, of minority groups such as Indians, blacks;

d. Our military industry doing fine, earning money selling arms;

e. The enrichment of a few and the impoverishment of the many, as if God discriminated and, in paradise, has prepared slums for the poor and elegant communities for the rich.

God loves the whole world. But God clearly shows a partiality to those who are suffering. Jesus declares himself present in the prisoner, but is silent about the imprisoners. He says he suffers with the hungry, but has no joy with those who are overstuffed with food. It appears that things are hard for the rich and the powerful from the perspective of the Kingdom of God. What do you think about this?

A practical suggestion: It is strange that we associate God's blessings with excess. Excess of food, of drink, of money. And what we do in celebrations, such as Christmas, is to give expression to this belief. But this seems to be more an idol of a society which gives great value to earning a lot and spending a lot. It would be possible to start an opposite movement: the churches could create celebrations based on poverty. Christmas: occasion on which, in Christian homes, meals are eaten with the poor. What could Joseph and Mary have eaten, in the stable? Jesus, obviously, must not have had disposable diapers.

To Pray

O God: Help us to see in our bodies and in the bodies of others the fleshly manifestation of your divinity. You chose to be and to live in a body like ours and all the pains and joys of our bodies are felt by the body of Christ. Help us to sense the beauty and the dignity of our bodies: the caresses of persons, of animals, of nature; the good taste of food; the smell of lush grass, of jasmine, of beans; the sound of the wind in the leaves of the trees, the noise of the ocean, the streams that play tag with the rocks, the berimbau,* the organs, the drums, the laughter; the body with gooseflesh in the cold wind; the taste of the jaboticaba fruit, of the grapes, of the mangos; the blue of the sea, the yellow of the ipe trees, the green of the pau-ferro bushes, the red of the parrots; and the capacity to play, cook, plant, walk, enjoy laziness in the hammock, in the blessing of your rest, which bids us do nothing, and to receive the grace of life, the power to love. All these things are your gifts through the gift of the body. And we thank you for this strange, terrible, marvelous power of our body, power which makes it spiritual and image of your love, power to feel pity and compassion, so that the sufferings of other bodies are felt as if they were our own. We suffer with those who suffer and know that when we suffer we are not alone. With this body we live the fraternity of love. We want you to enrich us, freeing us from the narrow limits of our skin, making our body fill out, to feel the pain of others. And so—open to joy and in solidarity in suffering, expressions of hope and love—may our bodies be living manifestations of the Body of Christ, destiny of the Universe. Amen.

*A one-stringed Brazilian folk instrument.

"DYING, WE ARE BORN"

*And Jesus answered them, "The hour has come for the Son
of man to be glorified. Truly, truly, I say to you, unless a
grain of wheat falls into the earth and dies, it remains alone;
but if it dies, it bears much fruit. He who loves his life loses
it, and he who hates his life in this world will keep it for
eternal life."*

John 12:23–25

*Then Jesus told his disciples, "If any man would come after
me, let him deny himself and take up his cross and follow
me. For whoever would save his life will lose it, and whoever
loses his life for my sake will find it. For what will it profit a
man, if he gains the whole world and forfeits his life? Or
what shall a man give in return for his life?"*

Matt. 16:24–26

God's desire is exquisite:
the entire universe, garden,
in the garden, smiling bodies with joined hands:
joy, pleasure.

Triumph of love, coming of the Kingdom, Christ in everything, everything a sacrament, to the ends of the creation. It
happens that this body, so lovely and friendly, is fragile.

Around it, the spectre of death. Amid the messages of life, messages of the end: sunset, fatigue, sleepiness, dry trunks, wrinkles, signs of old age, the cycles of the constellations, time that passes. And death, future, is established in our body, and begins to eat our flesh; animal ceaselessly gnawing. And, just as the locust is announced by its buzzing, death, still absent, is announced in a funeral lament which the body chants, monotonous and terrible: fear.

Fear is the song of death.
And the body, lovely, is twisted. . . .
Free, it crouches. . . .
Open, it is closed into a mask.

Temptation is established in the same place where fear dwells. And it presents itself as promise of life. If temptation didn't promise life, it would not fascinate, would not be temptation.

"—You surely will not die.
You will be like Gods" (Gen. 3:4–5).

Hope of each is hope of all: a magic fruit that changes our bodies of flesh and bone, fragile and mortal, into divine beings, forever, substances that never die, beyond the destiny that God gave us. If God had created us for death, we should be ephemeral, sad flashes of life and love, defeated from the beginning; useless sighs, empty gestures, lost words.

No, the promise of life flowered well in the midst of the garden: there was the tree of life, sacrament-fruits of eternal youth.

The condition of life was that we not seek it as a possession, but receive it as a gift. Serenely letting go in the hands of God. Confidence in the smile. Love casts out fear. Live day by day.

"Behold the birds of the air and the lilies of the field. Which of you, by being anxious, can add a single day to the course of your life?" Let go of all guarantees and all policies against the future. Useless our spiritual and moral savings. Lost the access to the tree of life.

"Abraham, Abraham, take your son, your only son, whom you love, son upon whom you have built your future, son who is continuation of your flesh, promise of immortality, and sacrifice him. . . . Let go of the magic fruit. Are you able to walk with empty hands?"

Justification by grace: life is given, as a surprise, unexpectedly. It does not sprout from our bodies, eaten by fear. But it comes to them, from the depths of a mystery, without our having done anything, riding on the wind, that blows where it wills. Bodies, kites held by love, powerless, wanting to make them fly, waiting for the wind. Theologians gave the name of grace to this uncontrollable and unpredictable wind in which our body-kites fly, playfully. Mysterious wind, beyond what we can, when we can not, despite our not being able, when our arm falls, impotent. And he comes, making the world spin and live, Spirit of God.

Life is lost when we no longer float at the mercy of God's goodness. Do you know how to float in water? You need to let the body go. Relax all over. Believe the water is friendly. And we let go, and the water takes and wraps us, like children.

But some are afraid. Letting go is impossible. Depend on another, be at someone's mercy: sentiments that give us vertigo. The body tenses. Thinks that its doing will make it float. It doesn't know that who does, sinks, and only who doesn't do anything, floats. God, great sea, ocean of love. It is necessary to let go. Sentiment of absolute dependence. That which is called faith, faith which is confidence. Abandon the struggle against death. Just gather in life, freely given, like manna. To keep nothing for tomorrow, as if goodness would not be given and the wind ceased blowing.

Battle with death: something that doesn't belong to us.
It is enough for us to receive life, as a gift.
Who wins, loses; who loses, wins.
Who holds on tight, ends up with nothing; who opens the hand, finds it is full.
Who holds on, falls; who lets go to be carried, flies, actually flies.

"They who wait for the Lord . . . shall mount up with wings like eagles" (Isa. 40:31).

TO THINK ABOUT

Have you ever tried to think, with awe and thankfulness, about the absurd possibility of your not being alive? That life is a gift, a miracle? That a mystery surrounds it?

You know that "justification by grace" is one of the central affirmations of the Christian faith. This means that life is not a problem to be solved. God does not keep count of our debits (good!) nor our credits (what a shame!). Read the parable of the Prodigal Son (which should actually be called "the parable of the righteous brother"!). Life and death are not problems, because a problem is something we have to solve. But life and death have already been solved by God. Now, we can only live them, as a gift, as grace.

The sense that life and death are problems results in our being immersed in anguish because we live as if everything depended on us. And, with this, we lose the freedom to live, the courage to risk, the tranquility to rest.

To Pray

My Father,
Make me sensitive to all the evidences of your goodness,
and may I, trusting in you,
free myself of the terror of death
and feel free to live intensely and happily
the life you have given me. Amen.

THE CRUEL BODY

For he grew up before him like a young plant,
  and like a root out of dry ground;
he had no form or comeliness that we should look at him,
  and no beauty that we should desire him.
He was despised and rejected by men;
  a man of sorrows, and acquainted with grief;
and as one from whom men hide their faces
  he was despised, and we esteemed him not.

Surely he has borne our griefs
  and carried our sorrows;
yet we esteemed him stricken,
  smitten by God, and afflicted.
But he was wounded for our transgressions,
  he was bruised for our iniquities.

                                                    Isa. 53:2–5a

*Then the King will say to those at his right hand, "Come, O
blessed of my Father, inherit the kingdom prepared for you
from the foundation of the world; for I was hungry and you
gave me food, I was thirsty and you gave me drink, I was a
stranger and you welcomed me, I was naked and you
clothed me, I was sick and you visited me, I was in prison
and you came to me." Then the righteous will answer him,
"Lord, when did we see thee hungry and feed thee, or thirsty*

and give thee drink? And when did we see thee a stranger
and welcome thee, or naked and clothe thee? And when did
we see thee sick or in prison and visit thee?" And the King
will answer them, "Truly, I say to you, as you did it to one of
the least of these my brethren, you did it to me."

Matt. 25:34–40

See how we are lovely, as the desire of God. So lovely that he created us to be mirrors. That his image and likeness should be reflected in us. And he made us from love, in love, for love, destined to walk with joined hands, sensitive to beauty, to goodness, to truth: our body became animate, alive, at the breathing of his Spirit.

But fear deformed us.
For who fears has fallen from love,
lost paradise, experienced the terrible loneliness of having to live life and death at the mercy of fate itself. And it is from this fear that cruelty is born.

No animal in the entire universe knows what this is. Sharks, cobras, scorpions, wolves, hyenas: all are capable of causing suffering, all are capable of killing. But they kill to defend themselves and to protect their young. Or they kill to eat.

We are the only ones with the strange capacity of killing for pleasure. The suffering of others makes us feel good. It is medicine for the soul. Among all the creatures of the universe we are the only ones with the horrendous possibility of torturing their own kind.

In the prison cellars, of course.
But torture assumes more subtle forms.
Defenseless victims: children, old people . . .

We invoke the human rights of prisoners. But who has ever seen the same rights invoked on behalf of children, against the cruelty of parents, or on behalf of the aged, against the cruelty of their children?

Frequently it will nestle quietly for an entire lifetime, in the subcellars of our soul, haunting our nightmares and firing our imagination. And we shrink, fearful, thinking of the violence of which we would be capable if the wild beast got loose. And not infrequently it happens. Now and then the tiger leaps and cruelty overflows, if not in irremediable gestures, at least in words.

The maid, in her little cell, in the rear of the apartment.
The beggar.
The unemployed, sitting hopeless on the park benches.
The poor.
Slum dwellers.
Migrants.

There is also that cruelty that breaks over entire social groups: concentration camps, for the Jews; refugee camps for the Palestinians; blacks enslaved; Indians decimated.

We do not look for the guilty.

We ask ourselves about the strange reasons that lead us to accept cruelty as normal. Which shows that it lives deep within us. We even admit that violence should be done against certain persons, as if there were a class of unfortunates that deserves to suffer. The guards in a prison locked the prisoners in a closed cell and threw in tear gas bombs. Besides fear and suffering, there were deaths. Peaceable citizens, in the barbershops, praised the deserved cruelty against the criminals. And from their speech there drooled, like spittle, a strange pleasure.

And there is cruelty against animals, our companions in this world of God.

And cruelty against the oceans, against the forests, against the rivers, against the land, against silence, gifts, sacraments of the body of Christ.

And war.

The military already have enough bombs to destroy our world ten times over. As if it were not enough to kill it once. An assassin who stabbed a fellow human being once, fatally, would be looked on with horror. If, after committing the crime, he punctured the body with a hundred more stab wounds, he would be considered a demonic beast. It happens that now the victim is not a person, it is life itself, the world, the body of Christ. It is not enough to stab it just once. Its death must be multiplied ten times over. And what do we do with the insane, who prepare this final ritual for the triumph of death? Do we send them in disgrace to uninhabited islands? Do we condemn them to the aridity of the deserts? No. We cover them with medals. And they sit down together with royalty, and in their honor the weaker bow in reverence.

And, despite all this, we still tremble with emotion at the sound of military marches and assuage our demons in the celebrations of violence that are served up to us, voluntarily, on the television. Whence this pleasure in seeing blood flow? Whence the pleasure in seeing bodies fall, cut down by bullets? Whence the pleasure in the contemplation of cruelty, whether its victims are the enemy or just animals?

The body of Christ is still crucified.
The creation is a groan.
And we, we groan also. . . .
"We complete in our bodies the rest of the sufferings of Christ,
    for the Kingdom."
Spears should be turned into plows.

But there is something more, something that has to do with
the mystery of this human heart, capable of hearing the voice
of God and capable of hearing the voice of the tempter, capable of planting gardens and of building concentration camps,
capable of choosing life or of choosing death.

TO THINK ABOUT

Talk about your fantasies of cruelty: the persons you defeat, attack, wound, kill. Do you never see yourself, in your fantasies, destroying things? As if someone put a machete in your hands and said to you, "Destroy!"

What provokes your sentiments of violence? Note that frequently our violence is not shown against others but against ourselves. This is why persons torture themselves with guilt feelings, even, in extreme cases, committing suicide.

To what kinds of cruelty are you now subjected? Who is responsible for them?

And the weak? The poor? The children? Old people? Abandoned adolescents?

Think about the problem of war. It seems so far off. But it isn't. Our future depends on the decisions of the few strong ones who consider themselves the owners of the world!

Think about a world from which cruelty had been banished: the end of torture chambers, the end of beatings, the end of hunger, the end of the exploitation of the weak by the strong, the rule of truth and of justice, children and old folk not afraid to cross the street, the destruction of all the armaments in a huge bonfire. Carnival of all humankind.

To Pray

O God, since the blood of Abel cried out to you, from the depths of the sand that drank it, this your land has been stained by the blood of men, spilled by their brother's hand, and all the centuries sob before the endless horror of war. The arrogance of those who sit in the seats of power and the greed of the strong have always led peaceful nations to slaughter. The hymns of the past and the pomp of the armies have always been used to inflame the passions of the people. Our spirit cries out to you, in revolt against this, and we know that our righteous indignation echoes in your holy wrath. Break the witchcraft that intoxicates nations with the will to battle, making of them deliberate instruments of death. Give us a calm mind when our own nation calls for vengeance and aggression. Strengthen our sense of justice and of the equal dignity of other peoples and races. Give, to those who govern nations, faith in the possibility of peace through justice and give to ordinary people a new and intense enthusiasm for the cause of peace. Bless our soldiers and sailors in their readiness to obey and their desire to respond to the call of duty. But, despite this, inspire in them a horror for war and may they never, ever, for the love of glory, provoke its outbreak. Father of all nations, gather your great family around a sense of one blood and of common destiny, so that peace may come to the earth, finally, and your sun may cause its light to shine in universal rejoicing on a holy brotherhood of all peoples.

Walter Rauschenbusch, *Prayers of the Social Awakening*

THE APERITIF OF THE FUTURE

All the created universe awaits,
with ardent expectation,
sentiments springing from the depths of the breast,
very near the heart,
that the veil that hides the children of God may be taken
    away.
Victim of frustration,
not by will but by destiny,
has not abandoned hope:
the whole universe will be freed of the chains of mortality,
    and will take part, with the children of God, in his
    brightness.
But, what do we know, so far?
The whole universe groaning, in all its parts,
as if it were in birth pangs.
And not it alone but principally us—
—we who have already tasted the aperitif of the Spirit,
the first fruits,
the first colors and perfumes,
the first smiles,
of the new world which comes of age.
Yes, we also wait, in the depths of our breast, for the
    moment when God will perform the magic of turning us
    into his children. And there, then, our body will be free.
    Freedom of the body: salvation!

It happens that, for now, we experience this salvation only in
  hope.
We see nothing.
If we saw, we would not need to hope.
Why should anyone have to suffer and hope for that which
  is already visible? But if we hope for something which we
  have not yet seen, in the very act of hoping we show our
  inner tenacity.

Rom. 8:18–25, paraphrased

The hand slides over the belly, looking for some difference.
But everything is the same, just as it always was; slender, skin
smooth. She smiles, however, and anyone who saw her would
not understand why she looks as she does at that common
womb, which she always saw. There is something magic
about the way the hands glide, as if in a caress. And the eyes
smile while the lips half open to croon, quietly, a lullaby.
That's because the woman knows things no one else knows.
She has received a notice, annunciation, word that came from
the future, a little piece of tomorrow. She is pregnant. Within
her, so small that from outside no one would suspect it, a little
child's body is beginning to form. And everything is different
for her. From the future there has come to her a secret flutter
of wings, and she no longer lives on the sustenance of the
bread of the present, but she feeds on the sacraments of a day
which is not yet born. It's from the future that life comes to
her: the hands sew, preparing the empty crib; the imagination
soars; and the dreams . . . Everything by hope, without seeing
anything. And the loved and awaited invisible one transfig-
ures the body which lives in another time.

Parable of what the Church is: those who have already experienced the aperitif of a new world. Paul doesn't talk about
aperitif. He talks about "first fruits." But who, among us, so

far from the miracle of the trees that give fruit, understands what he is trying to say? Imagine that before the abundance of flowers and of fruits, nature should send us, beforehand, samples of that which is to come. First fruits, messengers. And so we can, in anticipation, taste the good taste of that which is coming. They don't nourish us. They awaken the appetite. They make us desire, with more intensity. That's the way it is, too, with the aperitif which does not satisfy hunger but prepares the body for the food. It's like the caress which prepares the bodies for the union of the bodies in love.

Can this be?
Perhaps . . .
We, who try the first fruits
We, who experience the aperitif of the future
We, who were caressed by Someone, from the future.

How lovely is this image. It brings together the ideas of pleasure and of longing, of having enjoyed and of wanting more. So different from the weariness of those who have feathered their nests and pour themselves out, flaccid and sweaty, in the sun spots, to digest the rich foods. Which helps us to understand why it is so hard for the rich and the strong to enter the Kingdom. Their plenty makes them solid inhabitants of the now. They prefer obesity to pregnancy. Because pregnancy means a child, and a child is always a danger, an unforeseen, a resisting face. They come from within us but are not our property. They assume their destiny, subvert our space. The rich and the strong prefer slaves because they, unlike children, are subjugated bodies at the command of their masters. We are children of God, divine adventure, risk of rebellion.

We have been caressed by the Future . . .
And everything changed.

Because, in the same way the woman discovers she is pregnant, and begins to live to incarnate, by anticipation, the child who will be born, the Church is the community in which the future takes shape, first fruits, aperitifs, caress, of the future of the Kingdom.

And this future?
Salvation! Our bodies totally free.
Free of everything that causes suffering.

Free of chains, of fear. The eyes will no longer pierce, and none of us will have to hide, from anyone, either the nudity of our soul or the nudity of our body. Free for truth, for beauty, for love. Extraordinary, because our bodies will no longer react either to the evil eye, or the evil gesture, or the evil word. Possessed by the future, we will try to bring to life, in the present, that which was given us in hope. And this community of visionaries, of exiles, of pilgrims, of uprooted trees, will serve the world, in their own life, in sacraments of the Kingdom of God that is drawing near.

Church, community that is aperitif of the future. Do you believe this? Is it true? Might there be some community in which this is real? A scattered church, dispersed, one here, another there? Who are the persons with whom you would like to build the future?

What would be the reaction of people, outside the church, if she presented herself as a model, seed of the future? Why? Might there be some community of Christians who are helping people to be more hopeful?

What does the church do with our bodies? Should it be noted that it is through education that we learn to use our bodies in a certain way? Our position in the church, the attitudes we consider appropriate, the way we relate ourselves bodily to each other—this says something to us about the ideal the churches have for the body. Closing the eyes for prayer. What offends us more, violence or sex scenes?

The redemption of our bodies. This has to do with very concrete situations: working conditions, salary, health, house, water, yards, medical assistance, freedom to come and go, freedom from fear, knowing we are not going to suffer violence, guarantee of a dignified old age, possibility of leisure time. These are things that have to do with society as a whole. It is not an individual affair. It is the garden.

You will say that this has nothing to do with religion. But, how about the religious dignity of the body? And the solidarity and presence of the body of Christ? Is not a more just, a more gardenlike society, an aperitif of the Kingdom?

To Pray

My God, I don't know what to ask for. I tried to find my most ardent desire and didn't find it. I don't know what would make me happy. My heart is anxious, without rest and I don't know what name to give to my nostalgia. Not knowing where to go, what to do, what battles to fight, I feel intensely the temptation of the idols and of vanities. It is easy to take false paths, to prefer power over love, force over gentleness, violent reaction over gentle affirmation of goodness.

But I know that, despite all my stupidity, your Spirit loves me, frequents my dreams, my inward parts, the desires I don't know how to express, and intercedes for me and for all my brothers and sisters, in this world you have created, with groans too deep for words. Accept, my Father, my inarticulate groans as an expression of my petition. But, in my hunger, I need visible signs of your invisible grace. Serve me your sacraments, the first fruits of this Kingdom, nostalgia of our soul. I thirst for smiles, for gentle looks, for soft words, for firm gestures, by truth and goodness for victories, small though they may be, of justice. You know, Father, that it is very hard to survive in captivity, without the hope of the Holy City. "By the rivers of Babylon we sat ourselves down and wept, remembering Zion. . . ." Sing to us, O God, the songs of the promised land; serve us, in the desert, the manna; and give us the grace to play and leap on your rest days, as an expression of confidence. And may there be, somewhere, a community of men, women, old people, children, and nursing babies who may be a first fruit, an aperitif, a caress of the future. Amen.